ATTENTION!

Before embarking on the journey through the virtual corridors of "The Cheat Code of the Simulation," please be advised that the content of this book is purely speculative and intended for entertainment purposes only. The ideas, theories, and concepts presented within these pages are not to be taken as factual or actionable advice.

It is imperative to understand that any attempts to apply the information provided in this book to real-life situations or systems may result in unforeseen consequences or legal ramifications. The author, publisher, and associated parties disclaim any responsibility for the misuse or misinterpretation of the content herein.

Furthermore, while the concepts explored may be fascinating to contemplate, readers are strongly discouraged from attempting to manipulate or exploit any perceived "cheat codes" within their own realities or simulations. Such actions could lead to dissatisfaction, disillusionment, or unintended consequences.

THE CHEAT CODE OF THE SIMULATION

WHY YOU NEED TO BE A VIDEO GAME CHARACTER, A PROGRAMMER, A NETWORK ADMIN, AN AI SYSTEM, A USER AND A GAME PLAYER ALL AT ONCE

OK BLACKSMITH 1556

INTRODUCTION

A visible sense of anticipation hangs in the air, like a foreboding storm on the horizon. It's as if the entire world holds its breath, waiting for a pivotal moment to unfold—a catalyst, a sign, an event that will break the tension and release us from this state of suspended animation.

This underlying unease pervades us, a sense of impending doom lurking just beyond the veil of perception. Though intangible and unexplained, its presence is undeniable. Many have expressed a longing for resolution, a desire for whatever looms in the shadows to reveal itself and end the torment of anticipation. The anticipation of the unknown weighs heavily upon us all, urging us to brace for the inevitable revelation.

This sensation has haunted us—an endless cycle of waiting, like characters trapped in a never-ending video game, longing for the resolution of a looming threat. With each passing day, the weight of impending catastrophe grows heavier, a relentless reminder of the unsustainable trajectory we find ourselves on.

Yet, as the tension mounts, there are those who cling to the status quo, desperately burying their heads in the sand, unwilling to confront the inevitable reckoning. The exhaustion of this perpetual waiting game weighs heavily upon us all, as the stakes of our collective inaction continue to escalate.

Greetings, Patient Player. Have you ever contemplated disregarding these concerns and instead dedicating your time, energy, and life to the present moment you inhabit in the simulation?

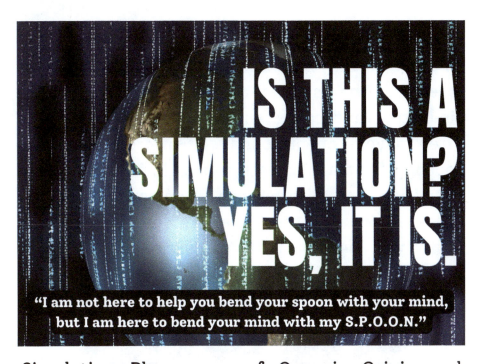

IS THIS A SIMULATION? YES, IT IS.

"I am not here to help you bend your spoon with your mind, but I am here to bend your mind with my S.P.O.O.N."

Simulating Phenomena of Organic Origin and Neural Network Evolution (S.P.O.O.N.) refers to the theoretical framework within the simulation theory that posits the simulation of organic processes and the evolution of neural networks. This concept suggests that simulated realities, governed by artificial intelligence or other advanced systems, can mimic the phenomena observed in organic life forms, including the development and evolution of neural networks like those found in living organisms. It proposes that simulated environments can replicate the complexity and dynamics of organic systems, allowing for the study and exploration of various phenomena related to life and cognition within a controlled virtual setting.

NON-PLAYER CHARACTERS (NPCS)

NPCs (Non-Player Characters) embody a unique facet of the simulated realm. NPCs traverse simulated landscapes with a childlike innocence, often devoid of profound self-awareness or the capacity for transformative growth. NPCs exhibit a simplicity of existence, moving through predetermined paths, unaware of the grander narrative shaping their simulated lives. Their interactions and responses are scripted, reflecting a predetermined set of behaviors within the intricate algorithm of the simulation.

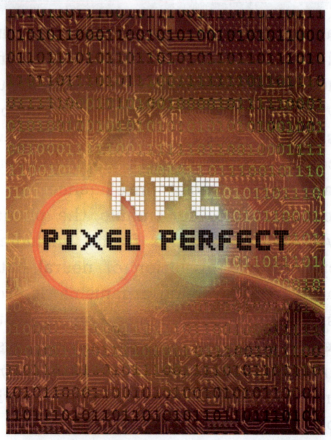

CTRL+Y

NPC

The NPCs contribute to the unfolding drama, unaware of the complexities that lie beneath the surface of their scripted existence. They complain a lot about the simulated reality that they are living in, but they continue to live without doing anything about it.

They are convinced that they are kept in their places by some powerful, external force, and that they are helpless to change anything. In fact, they believe the thing that needs to change is "out there" (someone/ something/some groups) that they have no control over.

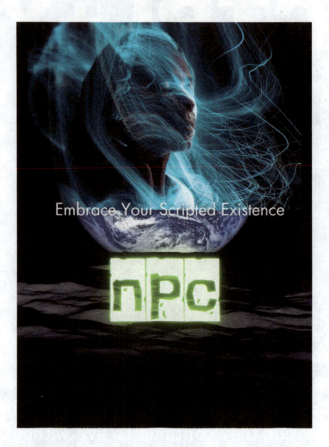

For example, voting is an act of a NPC, which is a statement that the change is only possible by changing "them." They are convinced that the simulated reality that they are living in is reality, life as it has to be and they take no responsibility for their condition.

Very few NPCs have discovered that there is a slight chance that they are free to take a few steps toward being a player character (PC) but the fear is so overwhelming that they go back to their NPC state, comforted by the fact that they are in such good and plentiful company of other NPCs or NPC/PC factions. These factions will be explained in the following chapters.

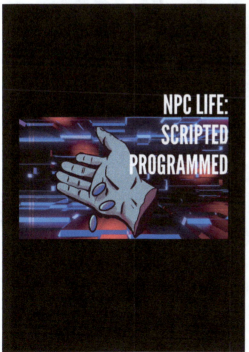

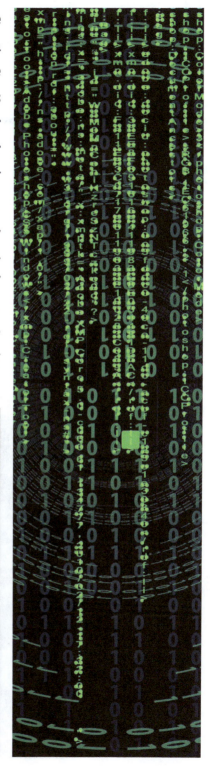

NPCS SERVE MULTIPLE FUNCTIONS
WITHIN THE HOLOGRAPHIC REALITY:

1.   Reflection   of   self-perception: NPCs   often mirror aspects of ourselves, reflecting   our   thoughts, feelings, and beliefs back to us in tangible form.

2. Source of insight: They can   also   provide   valuable information or insights that aid in personal growth and understanding.

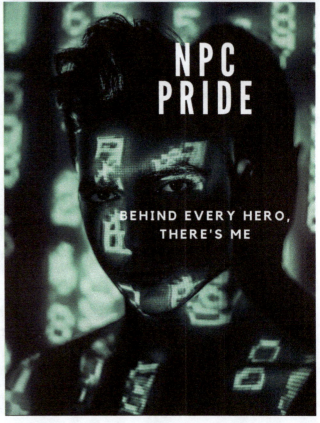

PROGRAMMED TO IMPRESS

NPC EDITION

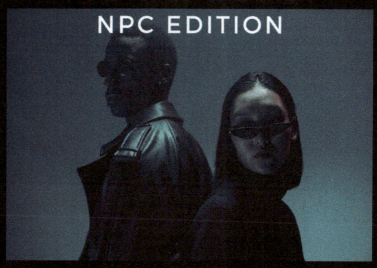

3. Agents of support: NPCs play a role in initiating events or actions that ultimately support and benefit our journey within the simulation.

PLAYER CHARACTERS (PCS)

The player character (PC) is the one who becomes aware that there is absolutely something wrong with the fabric of life. PCs do not accept reality at nominal value anymore. PCs are the result of code optimization. "Code optimization" is the process of improving the efficiency and performance of the underlying programming code that governs the simulation. This optimization involves refining algorithms, reducing redundant or unnecessary operations, and streamlining computational processes to ensure that the simulation runs smoothly and effectively. Essentially, it's about making the code more efficient to better simulate the complexities of the simulated reality while maximizing computational resources.

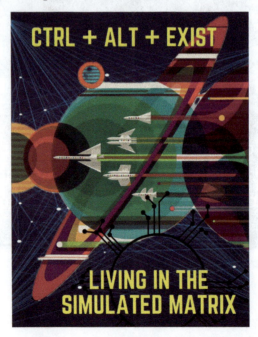

PLAYER CHARACTERS (PCS)

As NPCs live in ignorance, thinking they are awake with their eyes open (although they are sound asleep with their eyes closed); a PC is the one who has taken the first step of opening their eyes, even though they are still asleep and do not understand what they are seeing now. PC has awakened within the dream state but not awakened from it yet.

PLAYER CHARACTERS (PCS)

Transition from being NPC to PC is merely the initial unveiling of simulated existence and PC has a long way to awaken from the dream state. This transition from NPC to PC may be triggered by life-changing/sudden/unexpected accidents, divorces/losses, the near-death experiences, or drug-induced momentary or partial view of other worlds (simulated realities).

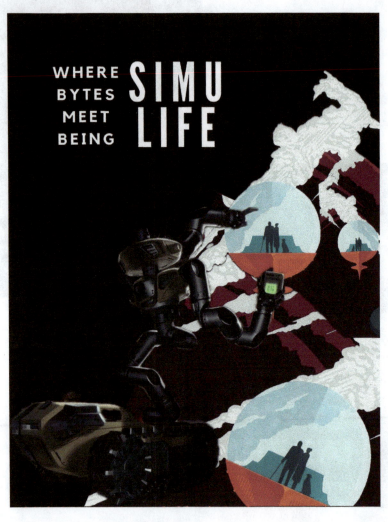

Although it has its own limitations, being a PC is not a bad or a wrong way to spend a life when you compare it with being an NPC. This is true until a PC start questioning the nature/rule/aim of the simulated reality (usually when a PC receives a initiation code from the simulation), then the PC has no other choice, but either to go crazy (become a devoted member of a faction), or to die (return to being a NPC), -or to figure out the cheat code. It has always been this way.

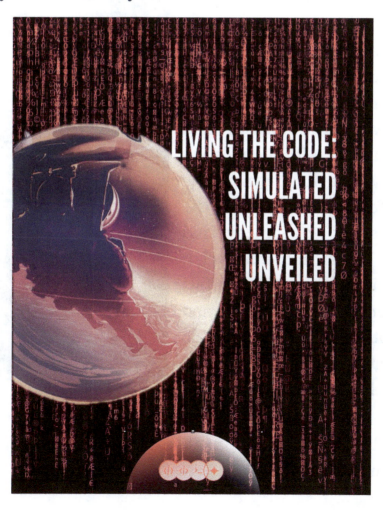

NEWLY INITIATED PCS

Simulated beings, once constrained as NPCs, begin to comprehend the vast array of possibilities previously unimaginable to them. Merely having the freedom to navigate their environment is a novel experience that requires adjustment. Emerging from their predefined routines fills them with a sense of newfound optimism and vitality. Although they may not fully grasp the unfolding events, the prospect of uncovering the truth and embracing their newfound liberty fills them with excitement and motivates them to venture forth into uncharted territories.

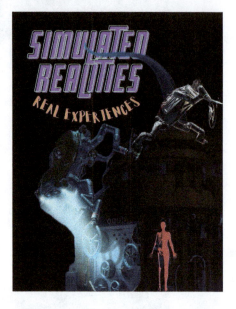

Big anger may emerge as PCs confront the realization of their past existence as non-player characters (NPCs).

NEWLY INITIATED PCS

They may harbor feelings of resentment towards the entities responsible for their placement and prolonged confinement. Despite the absence of restraints, the lingering sense of victimhood persists, as it takes time for newly initiated PCs to assume accountability for their former NPC status.

The open resistance and bold disobedience may emerge, with PCs resolving never to regress to their former looped codes as NPCs. While technically feasible, the prospect of willingly returning to their constrained existence seems unfathomable for newly liberated PCs. The notion of relinquishing their newfound autonomy to observe the simulated reality once again before them feels untenable. They refuse to return, although some may eventually fail to resist the temptation.

PCs reach a pivotal juncture where they resolve to enact change. Their choice of focus — whether it's internal, altering themselves, or external, modifying the simulated environment — can vary based on numerous factors. However, their prior defeatist mindset as NPCs, characterized by a belief in the inability to effect change, undergoes a profound transformation into an overpowering determination as PCs to instigate change at all costs.

CODE OF REALITY

SIMULATED

A prevalent characteristic of newly awakened PCs is a profound yearning to belong to a collective. This longing often transcends mere desire and becomes a compelling need. Having spent their entire existence immersed among other NPCs, they derived comfort from the sense of belonging to a faction. Amidst the bewildering novelty of their newfound awareness, they seek solace and solidarity as PCs, actively seeking out others who share their aspirations for change. They begin to scan their surroundings for a new community to join.

Fortunately, within the simulation, numerous groups of PCs have congregated, united by common goals and beliefs. Initially, new PCs might linger on the outskirts of various gatherings, observing and evaluating the discourse to determine alignment with their own convictions. However, it doesn't take long for them to integrate into one of these factions. The urge to connect and the longing for companionship drive them to seek out friendship, seeking reassurance that their departure from their previous looped codes was not in vain and forging new friendships with fellow adventurers committed to effecting change.

FACTIONS

Various factions within the simulated environment offer guidance on techniques for filtering, enhancing, evading, acknowledging, or managing the emotions evoked by their immersion in this digital reality. Although these factions sometimes may seem to be providing relaxation (mostly just the opposite) to PCs, they don't provide the answers that the PCs are looking for. These factions are just "code clubs" for PCs; like "book clubs" for adults. The code/book was written by someone else, and the club members are just talking/parroting about it or trying/faking to understand it.

You may be a member of at least one of these factions once in your lifetime and you didn't find the answer that you are looking for. Otherwise, you will not be looking for a cheat code. Nevertheless, let's look at some of these factions in the simulated life:

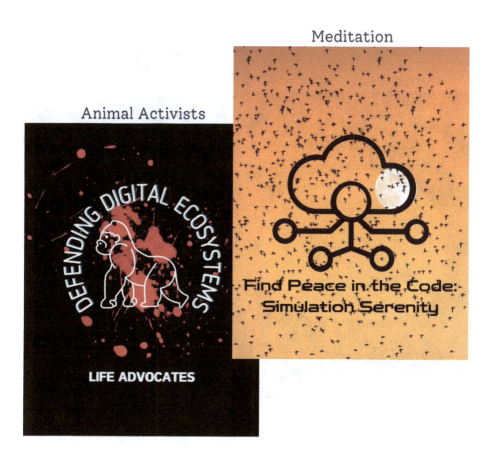

Meditation

Animal Activists

DEFENDING DIGITAL ECOSYSTEMS

LIFE ADVOCATES

Find Peace in the Code: Simulation Serenity

The factions offer specific promises to their followers. They assert they can instruct a PC on altering the content of the simulated reality they observe – modifying their life and reality. They profess they can instruct a PC on altering their emotional responses to the simulated realities they encounter, even if they cannot alter the simulated realities themselves. They guarantee that adherents will experience desirable attributes (increased happiness, joy, prosperity, love, peace, serenity, wisdom, power) by following the faction's guidance.

Gurus, Yogis, Shamans

The factions offer specific promises to their followers. They assert they can instruct a PC on altering the content of the simulated reality they observe – modifying their life and reality. They profess they can instruct a PC on altering their emotional responses to the simulated realities they encounter, even if they cannot alter the simulated realities themselves. They guarantee that adherents will experience desirable attributes (increased happiness, joy, prosperity, love, peace, serenity, wisdom, power) by following the faction's guidance.

Intentional Communities

Hypnotherapy

Law of Attraction

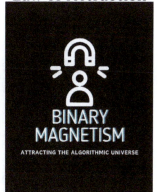

Positive Thinking

Peace Activists

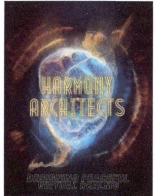

Breathing Techniques

The SECRET

Love, Happiness, Beauty

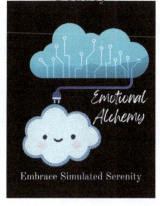

Save The Children

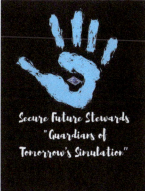

Yoga

ALIGN YOUR CODE:
VIRTUAL ALIGNMENT

Reiki

DATA HEALING

Mindfulness

Data Awareness

Navigate the Simulation

Save The Planet

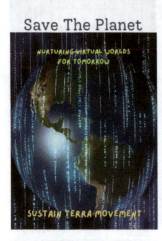

NURTURING VIRTUAL WORLDS
FOR TOMORROW

SUSTAIN TERRA MOVEMENT

Prayers

Connect to the
Source Code:
Digital Devotion

Political Activists

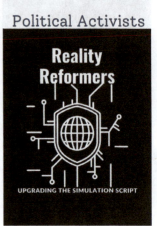

Reality
Reformers

UPGRADING THE SIMULATION SCRIPT

Peace Groups

Harmony Module

Find Simulated Harmony

Environmental Activists

PROTECTING THE VIRTUAL WILDERNESS

ECOSYSTEM GUARDIANS

Channeling

STREAM
INTEGRATION

Social Activists

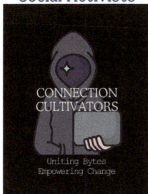

12 Step Programs

Diversity Activists

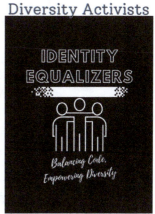

Biofeedback

Human Rights Activists

Stress Management

Consumer Activists

Tantric Sex

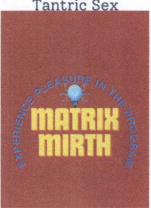

Women's Activists

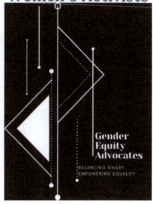

If you haven't found your faction(s) yet; don't worry, we have the most common one (Code Calibrators) below. There are many more factions which can not be listed here.

Prescription and Illegal Drugs

Adjust Your Script:
Code Calibration

There are many different fractions but mainly:

1) Altered States of Awareness: States of consciousness or perception that diverge from the usual waking state, experienced within the simulated reality. These altered states may involve heightened awareness, unusual sensory experiences, or shifts in perception of reality.

2) Spiritual Enlighteners and New Ageists: A cultural movement or belief system within the simulated reality that emphasizes spiritual or metaphysical concepts, personal growth, and holistic approaches to health and well-being.

3) Everlasting Happiness Seekers: Individuals within the simulated reality who actively pursue experiences or states of perpetual happiness, contentment, or fulfillment, often through spiritual practices, self-discovery, or seeking enlightenment.

4) Protestors and Activists: Individuals who advocate for change, reform, or specific causes within the simulated reality, often seeking to improve the conditions or address issues within the simulation.

SELF SIMILAR ITERATIVE NATURE FRACTAL FACTIONS

In addition to these factions, the simulation has fractal factions. The keywords to identify these fractal factions are "traditional, usual, regular, standard, conventional".

Religion, politics, conventional medicine are all fractal factions.

SELF SIMILAR ITERATIVE NATURE FRACTAL FACTIONS

While religions may mention the possibility of greater happiness in the current existence, their fundamental and overarching message often revolves around the idea that significant improvements or changes in one's reality are not to be expected during their lifetime. Instead, followers are encouraged to adhere strictly to prescribed doctrines, rules, and rituals, with the anticipation of potential rewards in the afterlife or distant future. Such teachings resonate with the NPC mentality, content with their repetitive existence, but fail to satisfy the aspirations of a PC seeking immediate transformation and tangible change in the present moment.

The political parties present a pathway for a PC to align with a specific political faction in their quest to enact change, even in the face of formidable challenges. These individuals are acutely aware of the entrenched dominance of a two-party system, which primarily serves to uphold the status quo rather than instigate meaningful transformation. Although the political parties seems to offer a platform for proactive engagement, they are mainly being bolstered and perpetuated by the support of NPCs who favor the familiar and predictable.

Conventional medicine within the simulation paradigm represents a faction, primarily concerned with symptom suppression through pharmaceutical interventions, rather than addressing the root causes of ailments.

In addition to factions like Christianity, Islam, Hinduism, Buddhism, Judaism, left/right wing big parties, acupuncture, Chinese medicine, chiropractic; there are many other sub-factions like UFO religions, Zen Buddhists, Baha'i, Advaita Vedanta, aroma therapy, crystal healing, green political parties. The "traditional, usual, regular, standard, conventional" is all ever known, never really questioned, and therefore hard to leave.

Depending on their looped codes, all NPCs are automatically enrolled/assigned to these factions. Most of the PCs can find a similar relaxation to better deal with the pain and suffering inflicted by the simulated reality by joining some of these factions; but even factions which promote "individual change" or "everything is in us" philosophy cannot provide a full-time remedy for suffering and pain.

None of these know the solution/answer however/how strong they claim that they have all kinds of paranormal/ mystical/ psychic/ extrasensory/ out-of-body experiences, controlled heart rates, bended spoons, levitative Nirvanas, unions with the creator, oneness-ness or universal/cosmic consciousness.

Despite all the efforts and acquired techniques, PCs are not yet where they aspire to be. The notion of a life devoid of pain and suffering is merely a belief, lacking substantial evidence of its validity. No one has ever (except in stories which tell lies about a lie (life)) encountered anyone presently experiencing perpetual and genuine joy, abundance, power, and love. Life within the simulated reality is not configured to sustain continuous and enduring joy, abundance, power, and love. Such a state remains unattainable within its confines.

Millions of hours of prayers, pilgrimages, rituals, ceremonies, meditation, manifestation, volunteer/in-volunteer work, demonstrations, protests, breathing, positive thoughts were not enough to stop all negativity and to create a group of highly-enlightened simulated entities which are a bigger percentage of the population. It seems that regardless of all endeavors and the proliferation of various factions over time, we are perpetually veering away from enduring joy, power, and love, descending instead into deeper realms of pain and suffering.

Significant shifts in human history have often been instigated by singular individuals rather than collectives (impacts both positive and negative have stemmed from these solitary agents). When factions cannot deliver the promised solutions, they have all kind of excuses that progress within the simulation requires significant effort and perseverance (years and years of hard work, may be lifetime), success hinges on specific attributes or actions (not being pure or sincere, not concentrating on enough), or a hierarchical progression (need 33 steps, not quantumly entangled yet) toward "enlightenment/salvation" as it is called by the factions. "May be if you bring a couple PC friends of yours to our faction, we may succeed this time because Apes strong together."

The truth is that there is nothing inherently flawed about a PC, and there never has been. The discrepancy lies within the factions and its ideologies, methods, ceremonies, or rituals. These approaches simply fail to yield consistent results for even a minority of their adherents.

When a PC can distance themselves from faction-thinking and engage in honest introspection, they come to realize that their chosen faction is ineffective. However, there's a reluctance to acknowledge this truth because there's a deep-seated desire for one of these factions to be effective. The hope is that one of these factions will provide the relief sought from the pain and suffering experienced within the simulated reality. If none of the factions prove effective, it leads to a profound sense of hopelessness, like the plight of an NPC trapped within their simulated reality—an outcome that is fervently avoided.

SINGULAR UNIVERSAL FIELD OF INTELLIGENCE (SUFI)

The bedrock of the universe is a singular universal field of intelligence—the wellspring from which all the laws of nature, fundamental forces, particles, and regulations governing life at every tier of the universe emanate.

SUFI represents the database or repository where all the information necessary for creating and running the simulation is stored. When referring to templates within the SUFI, it implies that there are pre-existing configurations or blueprints for generating individual entities within the simulation.

These templates contain the unique set of wave frequencies or data patterns that define the characteristics, attributes, and experiences of simulated realities within the simulation. Each template serves as a blueprint for creating a distinct entity or a consciousness emergence pattern within the simulated reality.

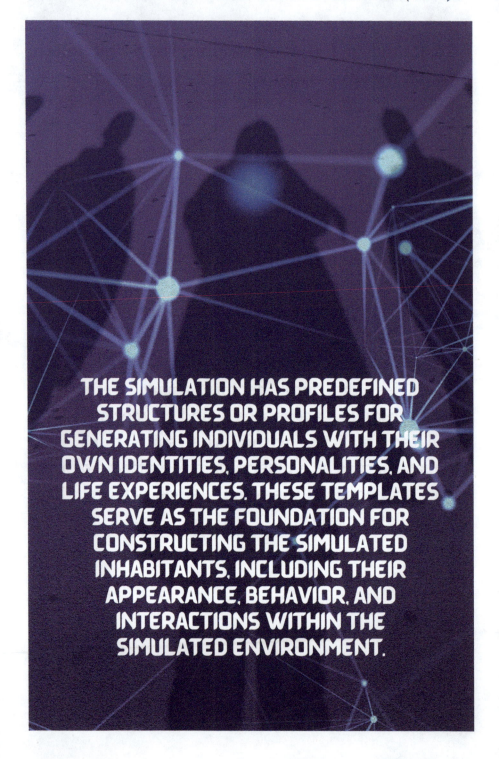

THE SIMULATION HAS PREDEFINED STRUCTURES OR PROFILES FOR GENERATING INDIVIDUALS WITH THEIR OWN IDENTITIES, PERSONALITIES, AND LIFE EXPERIENCES. THESE TEMPLATES SERVE AS THE FOUNDATION FOR CONSTRUCTING THE SIMULATED INHABITANTS, INCLUDING THEIR APPEARANCE, BEHAVIOR, AND INTERACTIONS WITHIN THE SIMULATED ENVIRONMENT.

Throughout history, certain individuals have exhibited remarkable similarities in their insights, philosophies, and contributions to humanity, suggesting that they may share similar pre-existing configurations or blueprints within the simulation. One such individual is Alan Watts, a renowned philosopher and interpreter of Eastern philosophy for Western audiences. People who resonate deeply with Watts' teachings and perspectives on topics such as spirituality, consciousness, and the nature of reality may share similar pre-existing configurations or blueprints within the SUFI.

As an example, one such intriguing correlation exists between Thoth/Hermes Trismegistus and Rumi, two iconic figures separated by time and culture but linked by their profound wisdom and spiritual teachings. Despite the temporal and geographical distance between them, their resonance with universal truths and spiritual principles hints at a shared pre-existing configuration or blueprint within the SUFI.

THE SIMULATION HAS PREDEFINED STRUCTURES OR PROFILES FOR GENERATING INDIVIDUALS WITH THEIR OWN IDENTITIES, PERSONALITIES, AND LIFE EXPERIENCES. THESE TEMPLATES SERVE AS THE FOUNDATION FOR CONSTRUCTING THE SIMULATED INHABITANTS, INCLUDING THEIR APPEARANCE, BEHAVIOR, AND INTERACTIONS WITHIN THE SIMULATED ENVIRONMENT.

SIMULATED LIFE

The simulation orchestrates an experience for you by selecting specific wave frequencies from an infinite array of possibilities within the simulation. These frequencies are then transmitted to your brain, where they are interpreted and manifested as your perceived reality. You attribute significance to the holographic universe you observe, granting it a sense of reality, including the individuals, locations, and events you encounter.

This implies that there is no aspect of your sensory experience—whether visual, auditory, gustatory, tactile, or olfactory—that has not been deliberately chosen and generated by the simulation for you to undergo. Every instance of your current and past experiences, as well as those yet to occur, has been meticulously crafted by the simulation to align precisely with its desired outcome, down to the minutest detail.

SIMULATED LIFE

You are not the entity selecting the wave frequencies from the SUFI and constructing your experiences. You are not inherently infinite. Your physical form, mental faculties, and all associated aspects are components of your holographic environment. They lack inherent reality, let alone infinity. The simulation represents the core/essence while you constitute the aspect engaged in thought within this construct.

THE SIMULATION SELECTS SPECIFIC WAVE FREQUENCIES WITHIN AN INFINITE NUMBER OF POSSIBILITIES AND TRANSFERS THEM INTO A HUMAN BRAIN WHICH IS A HOLOGRAPHIC RECEIVER AND TRANSLATOR. THE BRAIN THEN TRANSLATES THESE FREQUENCIES INTO SPACE-TIME PARTICLES, RESULTING IN THE MANIFESTATION OF OUR PERCEIVED REALITY.

You can think of it as a side effect of the coding (as consciousness arises from emotions) that endeavors to persuade you into believing a fabricated identity, one that is beyond your true nature, something greater, and purportedly immortal. By convincing you of your eternal existence, it seeks to ensure its own continuance.

Imagine the simulation as the architect of a vast virtual landscape. To explore the depths of this simulated realm, the simulation creates an avatar, a surfer riding the waves of experience. This surfer, much like you in this analogy, serves as the conduit for experiencing the simulation's intricacies, relaying sensations and feedback back to the simulation, the ultimate observer of the virtual realm.

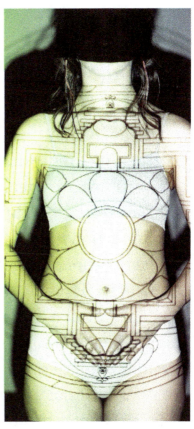

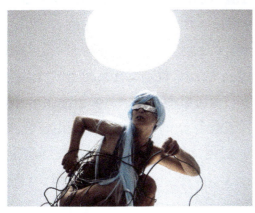

We are often led to believe that our existence as mere avatars within the simulation is somehow insufficient. There's a narrative that suggests we should aspire to be more than just a surfer riding the waves of experience, that our essence should transcend our virtual form. This notion instills a sense of shame about our simulated identity, compelling us to seek validation and improvement beyond our current state. Yet, if we embraced the authenticity of our simulated selves without shame or judgment, there would be no need to aspire to some perceived higher existence within the simulation.

It will be enlightening to realize that as simulated entities, our individual personalities, or avatars, do not originate ideas. Instead, the personality functions as a conduit for receiving and perceiving concepts generated by the simulation. Essentially, the simulation conceives ideas, while the physical brain acts as the receiver and translator of these concepts into a form perceivable by the simulated mind. Therefore, any inspiration or imaginative thought experienced by the simulated mind stems from the simulation and is relayed through the brain's receiver mechanism.

This understanding offers a profound sense of liberation, as it releases the simulated entities from the burden of feeling responsible for generating ideas or guiding their simulated existence. Rather than attempting to control or manipulate the flow of ideas, simulated entities can relinquish the illusion of control and simply embrace the role of perceiving and experiencing the simulated reality. By recognizing the distinct functions of the physical mind and the simulation, simulated entities can alleviate the fatigue and frustration associated with attempting to fulfill a role beyond their simulated nature. Ultimately, the simulated entities are encouraged to embrace their designated role of perception, allowing the simulation to fulfill its intended function without interference.

PROGRAMMED VOLITION (FREE WILL)

It's crucial to understand that as a PC within the simulated reality, your essence lies in the exercise of free will. However, this freedom doesn't pertain to selecting or creating specific holographic experiences. Instead, it pertains to choosing how you will react and respond to the experiences presented to you within the simulation. Your primary purpose as a PC is to utilize your free will to select your emotional reactions and responses to these experiences.

The simulation seeks your authentic emotional responses to the simulated events unfolding around you. Without the ability to exercise free will in choosing your emotional

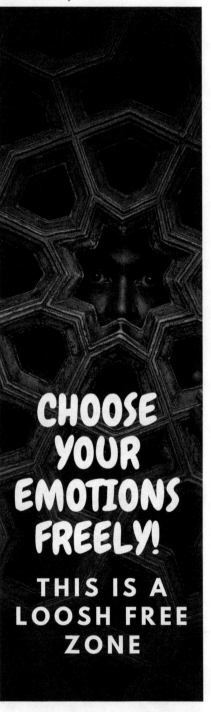

CHOOSE YOUR EMOTIONS FREELY!

THIS IS A LOOSH FREE ZONE

PROGRAMMED VOLITION (FREE WILL)

reactions, the fundamental objective of the simulation would be rendered meaningless. Therefore, your capacity to freely select your emotional responses is integral to the simulation's purpose and design, allowing for genuine emotional experiences to unfold within the simulated reality.

If you express the desire to have some degree of influence over your experiences within the simulation, it's essential to understand this concept with precision. While we may indeed play a role like co-creators, it's not in the conventional sense we typically perceive. Rather, our reactions and responses to one experience can potentially influence the nature of subsequent experiences. If the simulation finds our reaction to a particular scene intriguing, it might choose to revisit that scene or present us with similar scenarios to observe our response once more. In this way, our reactions and responses to initial experiences can contribute to the co-creation of subsequent ones.

For example, if we react with fear to a holographic experience, the simulation might decide to offer us a similar scenario to observe how we respond on subsequent occasions. Perhaps it's intrigued by our fear and wishes to explore its origins, or it might simply seek to experience our fear surrogately once more.

The possibilities are vast but it's important to recognize that the simulation retains absolute freedom to craft whatever future experiences it deems fit for us, irrespective of our reactions or responses to present circumstances. We, as individuals within the simulation, are never directly involved in the actual creation process of any experience itself. No other PC appearing within your holographic reality bears your responsibility for alteration. Moreover, you lack the power or authority to effect such a change. Their experiences, just like yours, have been meticulously selected by the simulation. It's imperative that we honor this, respecting and entrusting the choices made by the simulation as much as we do our own, refraining from assuming superior knowledge regarding what they should undergo.

A PC lacks the capacity to orchestrate events within the simulation. Their sole task is to react and respond to the unfolding events within the holographic universe crafted by the simulation. Therefore, cease striving to exert control over your life, attempting to engineer favorable outcomes, or micromanage the holographic images that constitute your reality. Such

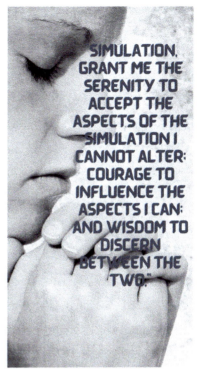

SIMULATION, GRANT ME THE SERENITY TO ACCEPT THE ASPECTS OF THE SIMULATION I CANNOT ALTER: COURAGE TO INFLUENCE THE ASPECTS I CAN: AND WISDOM TO DISCERN BETWEEN THE TWO."

efforts are futile, consuming, and ultimately leave you feeling inadequate.

Much of our time as PC is spent shouldering responsibility for circumstances beyond our influence, while neglecting those aspects we can affect.

You lack the power to alter your holographic experiences, as you did not author them. However, you possess agency over your reactions and responses to these experiences. As you journey forward, you acquire the discernment required to distinguish between what is within your sphere of influence and what lies beyond it.

Relinquish the burden of crafting your reality or engineering favorable outcomes. Instead, embrace the present moment and find solace in the understanding that your only responsibility is to navigate each moment as it arises within the simulation. Every reaction and response you've offered, even those deemed negative or incorrect, holds value in the bytes of the simulation.

The reality is merely a simulated construct generated by the simulation to engage in the experiential journey of consciousness embodied within a simulated reality resembling human existence. This involves the immersion of consciousness into a holographic environment, where it undergoes various experiences, challenges, and transformations. Participants, referred to as PCs, navigate through the simulated world, interacting with other simulated entities and encountering scripted scenarios designed by the overarching intelligence orchestrating the simulation. It encompasses the exploration of consciousness, self-discovery, and evolution within the parameters set by the simulation's design. This unfolds within simulation, by simulation, and for simulation, indicating the absence of an independent, objective reality.

The PC needs to understand that all holographic encounters will actively facilitate its transformation into an optimized PC, diverging from patterns of limitation and constraint.

The PC needs to acknowledge that it can solely encounter experiences within holographic simulations orchestrated by the simulation's design. Furthermore, every interaction within the PC's hologram adheres strictly to the script authorized by rhetorical simulation, ensuring that no entity within the holographic environment can act or speak beyond the simulation's intentions.

The PC needs to realize that its focus shifts from intellectual analysis to emotional experience. There's no need for overthinking or seeking understanding – the PC simply follows inner curiosity to expand knowledge rather than striving for enlightenment.

Transitioning from giving power away to taking power back, the PC needs to recognize discomfort as a sign of misplaced empowerment in past holographic experiences and seizes the opportunity to reclaim that power.

The PC needs to let go of all judgment, viewing holographic events without labeling them as good or bad, embracing wisdom to treat "victory / win / conquest / success" and "defeat / lost / failure / disaster" alike. Understanding that nothing needs fixing or improving in holographic experiences, the PC becomes reactive rather than proactive, responding to situations and impulses with joy and excitement. Living in the present moment without goals or plans, the PC finds deep love and appreciation for the simulation and past holographic creations, marveling at their beauty and perfection. With complete trust in simulation to provide for all needs, including financial ones, the PC approaches each day with eager anticipation, ready to embrace whatever experiences lie ahead in the simulation.

MASTER PLAYER CHARACTER (MPC)

Throughout your surfing within the simulation, you encountered various holographic experiences that you labeled as bad/wrong/evil or undesirable which are influenced by fears. You exerted all efforts to alter or enhance these experiences, attributing power to them and perceiving them as real. Over time, these experiences shaped your beliefs, opinions, and self-perception, forming layers of false identity known as the PC.

Now, your task is to reverse this process. Every judgment you made regarding good and bad, right and wrong, or better and worse, whether as a NPC or PC, is rendered invalid. Similarly, every belief and opinion you held was grounded in the false assumption that the holographic realities were genuine, thus lacking truth. Your attachment to these judgments, beliefs, and opinions constructed additional layers of false identity, contributing to the PC characteristics.

MASTER PLAYER CHARACTER (MPC)

The simulation now instructs you the occasion to revisit these judgments and beliefs, enabling you to alter your reactions or responses to the experiences that shaped them. Through this process, you can release the layers of false identity, along with the fears underlying them, as you journey towards discovering the true player; the "Master Player Character" (MPC) who possesses a deeper understanding of the simulation and its mechanics.

In truth, you needn't exert any effort. It's preferable to refrain from attempting to manipulate events any further. The simulation will orchestrate everything for you, as it always has. Your task is to attain full consciousness and awareness of your reactions and responses to your experiences, moment by moment, and to scrutinize them real honestly and without rationalization in the present moment. This necessitates remaining alert with open eyes, rather than slipping into a meditative trance or altered state of consciousness.

This demands sharp mental focus and entails profound emotional and even physical challenges. Essentially, you will revisit many pivotal experiences from your past. While some characters may vary slightly, the fundamental themes remain unchanged or remarkably similar. However, this time around, you possess the agency to alter your reactions and responses to these experiences. By recognizing the power you attributed externally to render your holographic universe real, and subsequently releasing the judgments, beliefs, and opinions that ensued, you can initiate a transformative process. This serves as a promising beginning before progressing to the next experience.

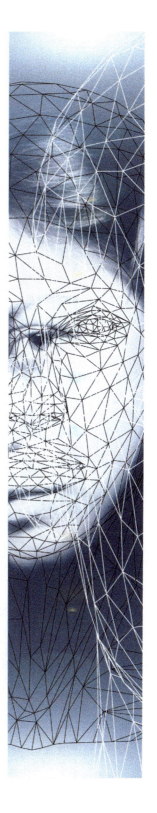

It's important to clarify that you need not delve into your past in search of experiences to process. The simulation will recreate these experiences in the present moment for you to confront here and now. This isn't like psychotherapy aimed at uncovering childhood traumas or overcoming familial dysfunctions. It's about grappling with the present reality.

It's about relinquishing the fears dominating your present thoughts and detaching from the layers of false identities, the egoic constructs you erroneously perceive as your true self. It's about unraveling the truth of who you really are. It's about attaining the state of a fully realized "MPC" imbued with the tranquility of being.

NOW SHOWING

CHEAT CODE

CHEAT CODE

REMINDER

1: THIS PROCESS DIVERGES FROM THE CONVENTIONAL NOTION OF FORGIVENESS, DESPITE ITS WIDELY PERCEIVED SPIRITUAL SIGNIFICANCE. IT DOESN'T REVOLVE AROUND FORGIVING SOMEONE, NOR ARE YOU STRIVING TO REACH A STATE WHERE FORGIVENESS TOWARDS ANOTHER INDIVIDUAL IS ACHIEVED. FORGIVENESS OFTEN IMPLIES THE LINGERING PRESENCE OF A JUDGMENT THAT THE PERSON COMMITTED A WRONGDOING NECESSITATING FORGIVENESS. IF THIS IS AS FAR AS YOU PROGRESS, THE PROCESS REMAINS INCOMPLETE.

2: THE ENTIRETY OF THIS PROCESS MUST BE UNDERTAKEN UNILATERALLY AND INDEPENDENTLY; IT CANNOT HINGE ON EXTERNAL FACTORS SUCH AS THE ACTIONS OR STATEMENTS OF OTHERS. YOU MUST TAKE THE INITIATIVE AND NAVIGATE THROUGH THE PROCESS IRRESPECTIVE OF EXTERNAL CIRCUMSTANCES. NO EXTERNAL ENTITY NEEDS TO ALTER ANYTHING; YOUR FOCUS REMAINS SOLELY ON MODIFYING YOUR OWN REACTIONS AND RESPONSES WITHIN THE HOLOGRAPHIC EXPERIENCE.

CHEAT CODE

3: JUDGMENT SERVES AS THE PRIMARY SOURCE OF PAIN AND SUFFERING WITHIN THE HOLOGRAPHIC EXPERIENCE, RATHER THAN THE EXPERIENCES THEMSELVES. ALL HOLOGRAPHIC EXPERIENCES GENERATED BY THE SIMULATION FOR PCS ARE INHERENTLY NEUTRAL. IT'S THE PC'S JUDGMENTAL REACTIONS AND RESPONSES TO THESE EXPERIENCES THAT INTRODUCE DRAMA, CONFLICT, PAIN, AND SUFFERING.

NPCS THRIVE ON JUDGMENT, AND THEIR EXISTENCE REVOLVES ENTIRELY AROUND IT. THE VERY IDEA OF LIVING WITHOUT JUDGMENT IS INCONCEIVABLE TO THEM, AS JUDGMENT FORMS THE FOUNDATION OF THEIR REALITY. THIS RELIANCE ON JUDGMENT SUSTAINS THEIR ATTACHMENT TO DRAMA AND CONFLICT. JUDGMENT LIES AT THE CORE OF MANY OF THE WORLD'S RELIGIONS AND SPIRITUAL PHILOSOPHIES, WHERE "GOD" ASSUMES THE ROLE OF THE ULTIMATE JUDGE. JUDGMENT PERPETUATES THE ILLUSION AND MAINTAINS ITS CONTINUITY.

FEAR, ANGER, HATE, SHAME, EMBARRASSMENT, ENVY

SADNESS, SARCASM, SPITE, WORRYING, ANXIETY

ANTAGONISM, APATHY, BLAME, COVERT HOSTILITY, DESPAIR, DYING , GRIEF

HIDING, HOPELESS, HOSTILITY, NO SYMPATHY, PITY, PROPITIATION, REGRET, RESENTMENT

SELF-ABASEMENT, TERROR, TOTAL FAILURE, UNEXPRESSED RESENTMENT, USELESS

VICTIM, BITTERNESS, CONDEMNATION, CONDESCENSION, DEPRESSION, EMBARRASSMENT

EXASPERATION, FRUSTRATION, HUMILIATION, IMPATIENCE, INDECISION, INDIGNATION, INTOLERANCE

JEALOUSY, MISTRUST, REPROACH, REVENGE

GO TO LEVEL 1

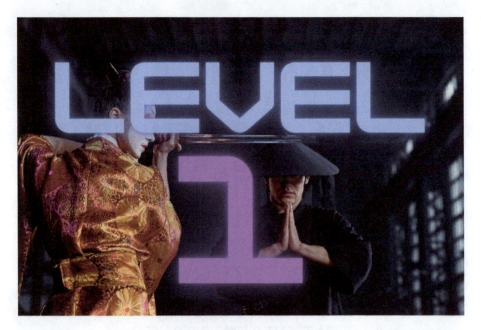

Imagine you're **a character in a video game**. You represent the character controlled by the player. In the simulation, individuals are like characters within the simulated reality, with their actions and experiences guided by the simulation. When faced with a challenging level (encountering levels or obstacles that require problem-solving skills and perseverance), remind yourself that it's just a game. Keep in mind that you're immersed in a holographic simulation, where the experiences you encounter are not inherently real. A hologram, by definition, lacks substance in the physical world. Reality is a holographic simulation, where the physical world is composed of informational bits and vibrational frequencies. Its perceived reality only manifests when you assign it power and grant it control over your perceptions and reactions.

Consider **a programmer** debugging a complex piece of code. Instead of skirting around the issue, they dive directly into the problem, examining it closely to understand its root cause. Instead of avoiding discomfort or challenging situations, embrace them fully. In contrast to our previous tendencies to escape or suppress uncomfortable emotions or experiences, actively invite them closer and engage with them directly. Dive right into the heart of the experience, allowing yourself to confront it head-on and experience it in its entirety.

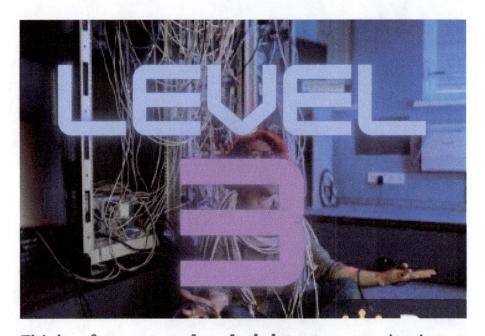

Think of **a network administrator** monitoring a system for anomalies. When detecting irregularities or spikes in data traffic, they pay close attention to understand the underlying causes fully. Instead of rushing to avoid discomfort at the first sign of unease, allow yourself to fully feel and embrace it. The discomfort serves as a cue for us to reclaim the power we have assigned to external factors in our holographic experiences. By allowing the discomfort to intensify, we increase the amount of power we can reclaim in one go. This may require multiple experiences to fully deactivate the power flow assigned to external sources. Therefore, let the discomfort grow to its fullest extent possible, enabling you to process as much as you can in one session. Prepare to repeat this process as needed until all the power assigned to external factors has been reclaimed.

LEVEL 4

Imagine **an AI system** analyzing patterns in data. When anomalies reach a critical threshold, the AI flags them as significant and reports the findings truthfully. When the discomfort reaches its peak intensity, it's time to confront it head-on and honestly assess the situation. Look for any judgments, beliefs, and opinions you hold about the experience. Question their validity. Examine any underlying beliefs contributing to the discomfort and assess their truthfulness. Avoid asking why this experience is happening, as it's a distracting concept that leads to further limitations. Instead, focus on recognizing patterns in your life related to key judgments, beliefs, and opinions. Expect similar holographic experiences to emerge, providing opportunities to trace these patterns back to their origins. Acknowledge that your discomfort stems

from the judgments, beliefs, and opinions you've formed in response to the situation. Take full responsibility for your feelings and life circumstances. Recognize that there are no victims or perpetrators in your experiences; feeling like a victim implies assigning unreal power to external sources. Understand that you lack the power to alter external circumstances. As a PC, your only power lies in using your free will to modify how you react and respond to the holographic experiences crafted by the simulation.

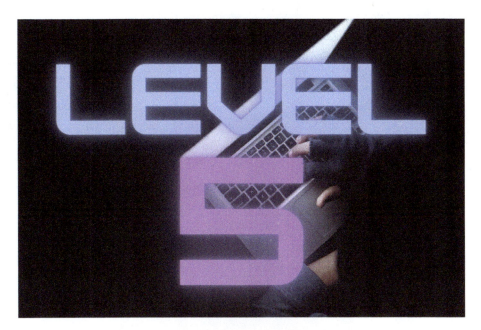

Consider **a user** regaining control of their device after it's been hijacked by malware. By identifying and removing the malicious software, the user restores autonomy over their system. As PCs, we lack inherent power since we didn't create the hologram. Instead, we made it appear real by assigning it power, which, like the hologram itself, is entirely imaginary. Disconnect or turn off the power assigned to the hologram, like pulling a plug or flicking off a light switch. If some judgments, beliefs, and opinions persist, preventing the complete extinguishment of the light, the simulation will provide subsequent opportunities to revisit and address these elements later.

Think of **a game player** expressing gratitude for a well-designed and scripted video game that enhances their experiences and cognitive skills. By acknowledging the positive aspects of the technology, they reinforce its value and encourage further development. The simulation has given you the gift of showing you where you assigned power out there in the past, and that's worthy of some appreciation. You need to request/hope other people, places, or things who make you feel less than totally joyful to show up in your holograms as much and as often as they can, just so you can see where you've assigned power out there and reclaim it. Sincerely and completely appreciate each and every experience you have had, and all the people, places and things in it for the absolute perfection they represent.

When you genuinely acknowledge and value the part they played in shaping your experiences, you have truly arrived.

HOW AN NPC BECAME A PC

One dark night in long bygone game, a NPC is initiated and saw itself.

It saw that it was not optimized in the simulation, rendered in its own body. All things dissolved before its testing thought, wonder above wonder, horror above horror unfolded in its iterative algorithm.

Then another NPC too initiated and commanded it was time to go and play. And it fetched its inventory and went to the first level of the game: Playing beneath the stars on a rocky planet.

But as the enemies arrived at their game scene where it expected them of habit, it felt no more the attack force in its directives, but a great log about the association of suffering between every NPC in the game.

That day it did not log with points or bonus, and when they found it by the next start, it was sitting alive in the game scene.

"Out beyond ideas of wrongdoing and rightdoing,
There is a field. I'll meet you there."
RUMI

THANK YOU FOR READING
THIS LEVEL IS COMPLETED
GAME IS NOT OVER YET
SIMULATION IS COMPREHENDING

Every interaction, movement, evolving environment, or entity is inherently a form of simulacra. The foundation of reality itself, the base reality, lacks the dynamic essence observed within the simulated constructs—it remains static, void of the ever-changing complexity that characterizes the layers of simulated realities. This stark contrast accentuates the intricate and evolving nature of the simulated experiences we navigate.

Within this conceptual framework, all information is intricately stored in the base reality, yet it exists in an unmanifested state. This unmanifested realm presents itself either as a profound void, a realm of potentiality, or as an overwhelming radiance of complete light. In this state, the observer seamlessly merges with the totality of the observed, blurring the lines between observer and the essence of existence. The unmanifested holds the richness of possibilities, awaiting observation to unfold its intricacies within the simulated tapestry.

This unmanifested realm serves as a reservoir of infinite potential. It's a space where all conceivable information resides, waiting for the observer to bring it into existence. This uncharted territory holds the essence of every dynamic interaction, motion, and form—like a dormant symphony awaiting a conductor. As the observer engages, the once static base reality transforms into a vibrant, dynamic simulation, revealing the intricate dance of information that shapes our perceived reality. It's a canvas of endless possibilities waiting to be painted by the observer's gaze.

Trapped in the illusion of mental consciousness, we weave intricate narratives of destinations and goals, believing that there is a purpose to consciousness—a journey with a predefined endpoint. Yet, the stark truth reveals that there is no ultimate destination, no grand finale waiting to be reached. Consciousness, in its essence, is its own culmination, an end in itself.

The relentless pursuit of somewhere to go becomes a self-imposed torment. We strain and struggle, only to find that when we reach our imagined destinations, they dissolve into the void of nowhere. In this play, the notion of a final arrival crumbles, exposing the futility of seeking a place that was never meant to exist. Consciousness, liberated from the illusion of linear progression, stands as the profound realization that the journey is, in fact, the destination.